51 Stupid Questions People Ask or Say to Veterans!

by

Fred "Bo" Dunning

INTRODUCTION

One of the most significant issues that military veterans struggle with is the assumptions people make about them. Just coming up to a veteran asking personal questions, and yes, questions about their military service are private. Their response depends on the question and the veteran. If you are going to ask the question, you might need to prepare for the reply. Sometimes, the question will not get the expected positive response, and civilians can become dumbfounded or offended. Most veterans do not like to share experiences because they fear judgment for what they had to do. There are so many stereotypes and misnomers surrounding veterans that they cannot know what will come out of a civilian's mouth.

The best thing is to get to know the veterans before quizzing them on their military service. Until you have a relationship with a veteran, you will not find out what they have or have not done in their life. The first thing people need to remember is, not all veterans are the same.

Every veteran is different, and it starts with the branch of service. The Air Force has a distinct role

from the Army, the Marines are separate from the Navy, and the Coast Guard is overlooked. All branches have their quirks. None of the military branches are alike. The boot camps, regulations, and uniforms are all different, and every service believes there the best. Veterans have various jobs depending on their branch. Each branch has a unique mission. There are a lot of differences in veterans, especially when it comes to personal experiences.
There are various and differing experiences veterans face causing them to differ in opinion and personality. Someone raised in the Appalachian Mountains will vary from someone from Oregon. Each will look at their military experience from a different lens based on their experiences before joining the military. Some veterans have seen combat, where others have not. Some have traveled, and others have never left the local area they were raised except to attend Bootcamp. Each different experience changes a veteran giving them a unique perspective of their life.

Sometimes those who have not seen combat have shame and guilt surrounding their lack of fighting in a war, knowing that others have fought and risked their lives, and they had not. The guilt of not seeing combat does not limit the judgment to civilians. Other veterans pile on because someone had not seen action or deployed. The Marines even have a term for it. They are called "Boots." This shame and guilt are especially true for some Vietnam-era veterans sent to Germany instead of Vietnam. A lot of combat veterans have their own struggles they deal with daily. Some veterans might have lost friends to combat and blame themselves for not being there to protect them. Some who survive combat have survivors' guilt. A group of veterans who have seen action together is intimate with those there with them that most people cannot understand. That is why they would rather be with and talk to their buddies instead of their families. Some veterans who have traveled the world have a different take on the world and life in general. Traveling the world gives you an outlook on life that others cannot fathom unless you have traveled yourself. This also gives them a sense of what is essential and what is not. After you have seen combat and been to third-world countries, some things just do not seem vital to life.

Veterans have a different take on life, especially combat veterans. No one goes to war and comes home the same. Almost all veterans look at life differently and have a darker sense of humor than most civilians. Veterans have a morbid way of looking at life that few civilians will understand. As veterans, we can pick on each other, make inappropriate comments about each other and their branch of the military. We are taught to dehumanize the enemy, and that comes out at times. We can be un-couth and make derogatory terms about a different race or ethnicity, which is required to kill someone. We will protect each other no matter the branch of service. We can fight with each other and often do. Still, an outsider will get the full blow from all veterans if they feel any veteran is threatened by a civilian.

But there are a lot of similarities too. We struggle with civilians and how they act. Often veterans feel that many civilians have no honor, loyalty, and dedication. Often veterans feel civilians are not in it for the greater good. They are in it for themselves. Basically, for the most part, veterans do not trust that civilians will have their backs. A civilian's trust can be attained by veterans. Still, it takes time, effort, loyalty, and a faith that many civilians do not understand or take the time to achieve.

Often, veterans look back at their lives and ask themselves, what have I done, or how things could have been done differently. Veterans also have different experiences than most civilians. Asking questions as if all veterans have seen combat or have Post Traumatic Stress Disorder (PTSD) is quite presumptuous. Having a perceived notion says more about you than about them.

Being asked stupid and disrespectful questions is why some veterans do not acknowledge their military service. In 37 years of being in the military and working with veterans as a therapist, I have compiled a list of 51 inappropriate questions/comments I have heard or been asked by a civilian.

No. 1
Thank you for your service

We all know that those who make this comment have good intentions. Many times, I find that it is what veterans say to other veterans. But you must be aware of what saying thank you for your service could bring up. For some thanking them for their service is thanking them for breaking their moral code. Veterans can feel that a civilian has no way of knowing or understanding what the veteran had done and what they are thanking them for. When people thank me for my service, I usually feel uncomfortable and awkward. The term has been said so often that it has become meaningless and feels like it is being politically correct. It's like saying, how are you doing? You really do not want to know. It feels like an empty gesture. Some veterans also feel it is a civilian's way of dealing with their guilt for not enlisting. The best way to thank a veteran for their service is to use the rights they fought for. Protest when necessary, use your voice, and most of all, VOTE. Also, it might be a good idea to start a conversation about their service without asking stupid questions. Show sincere interest in their military service. Ask them where they were stationed, what branch they were in, when they were in, ask benign questions. Many veterans are still healing. The healing power of connection, conversation, and purpose help bridge the gap between veterans and civilians. Do not be discouraged if they do not engage. Many veterans just want to be left alone, especially if they are suffering from PTSD. Some veterans might think, OK, here comes the stupid questions when you engage. Show sincere interest and don't ask stupid questions.

No. 2
Did you kill someone?

I do not know where to start with this question. First off, that is none of your business. Of all the questions people could ask, this is one of the most common and inappropriate questions possible. This is an assumption that all military veterans have served in combat. If they have been to war and had to kill someone, you could be causing the veteran pain and anguish for your own curiosity. I genuinely do not understand why someone would be so selfish to settle their own curiosity by asking this question. This question shows that you allow your curiosity to supersede the wellbeing of someone who has risked their life for your freedoms. Those who have had to kill someone can make them relive what they had to do. This question can cause a veteran to become a smart ass, get angry, lash out, shut down, or go into depression. They can feel shame, guilt and cause mistrust of civilians. The worst is the increased risk of suicidal thoughts because of your cluelessness or curiosity. If you ask this question, don't be offended by their answers. I have heard many answers to this question, and none of them have been good. Most have been sarcastic. A lot of veterans will respond something like, not yet... should I start with you? I have also heard... I was in Nam... what do you think?

Any way you look at it, this is a question you should never ask a veteran.

No. 3
How many people have you killed?

Again, this is one of the most inappropriate questions to ask. Most combat veterans do not have a number unless they are a sniper. Most combat is chaotic, and if they wanted to answer, most could not give you a good number because they do not know. There is a lot of spray and pray in combat, and it is hard to tell if your suppression fire killed someone. I have got a question for you. Have you walked up to your local gang member or police officer and asked how many people they had killed? Just because someone is a veteran and you assume that they serve in combat does not make them someone who has killed before. So many veterans who serve in combat zones do not know nor do they care how many of their enemies they killed. Their focus was trying to save those in their unit and themselves. Like question #1, it too can cause a host of emotions and anger that you would be so insensitive to ask a question like that to them. If you ask this question, do not be offended at their answers or how they react.

No. 4
How could you kill someone?

This is a question that just screams that you're judging me. The best answer is because the enemy was trying to kill my people or me. This question causes the veterans to feel they are being judged and can cause them to question their morality or judgment. It is difficult enough to deal with the moral injury of killing someone without you asking a question like that. In war, people are killed. It is just a part of it. I guess the short answer is would you kill someone if they were threatening your family or friends and you have the means to do something about it. That is the situation combat veterans are placed in. Most people, both civilian and military, can kill someone if the situation warrants it. When someone is shooting at you or your family, and you have the means to fight back, wouldn't you? And if the answer to that question is no, then the next question I would ask is why you would not.

No. 5
What did it feel like to kill someone?

I do not know, let me see... Killing someone, even having to kill the enemy, is something you never forget. You bring the pain and guilt home with you, and you are never the same. It never leaves you as you age. People learn to live with it, but it can shape your life and lead you down a dark path. By asking this question, you are asking someone to relive possibly the worst day of their life. Why would you do that? If you are curious, get to know the veteran, and they might tell you in conversation, but I doubt it. I know people who do not even acknowledge they killed someone to their spouse. What makes you think you deserve to know. If you are just that selfish that you feel the need to ask that question, please just go away.

No. 6
Did you kill any women or children?

I do not know how many ways this can be inappropriate. As stated before, they might not know. Again, why would you ask this question? If they did, it brings up the shame and guilt that is present in moral injury. Our society frowns on killing anyone, especially women and children. But my question is would you kill them if they were shooting at you? Have on a suicide vest? or threatening your unit or family? The enemy does not look at life the same way Americans do in some parts of the world. Often they use women and children, so our soldiers hesitate. Then they use that to their tactical advantage. It is also a way to conduct psychological warfare because they know Americans value the lives of women and children. To them, the child or woman might be expendable. I have a client who had to shoot an 8-year-old girl with a suicide vest on. He lives with that every day and cries in my office because of it. Why would you even think to ask him a question like that?

No.7
Did you see any dead bodies?

Again, this is a considerable jump in assumptions. If you are talking to a combat veteran, it is safe to assume the answer is yes, so do not ask. If you are talking to a non-combat veteran, the answer is probably no, so again do not ask. Some veterans that are non-combat veterans have some guilt over not seeing combat. By asking that question, it might cause the veteran to be triggered or go into a depression, especially if they lost a friend from battle. You are asking them to relive some dark days in their lives and could cause them to be triggered and want you to be the next dead body they see.

No. 8
Did you lose any friends?

Why would you ask them to relive this if they did? It can bring up a lot of emotion in someone who has. Some feel the loss of a friend is their fault. I lost my best friend to an accidental drug overdose, and I get emotionally charged when I think about him. I cannot imagine losing someone I was or am close to seeing them die in combat and having to relive what you cannot unsee. I know someone who must live with the loss of his whole squad while he was overwatch. His team went into a booby-trapped building, and the building blew up while he was watching. There are a lot of combat veterans who experience similar events. This question can stir up the shame and guilt of not doing anything about the situation. It also reminds the veteran that they are alive, and others are dead, triggering survivors' guilt. My question is, why would you ask that? Why do you care?

No. 9
Do you think God could ever forgive you for killing someone?

WOW! Yes, people do ask this question. Well, do YOU think God will forgive you for your drinking...adultery...or just being stupid? This question usually comes from someone so oblivious to the world that they believe it is OK to question someone's reasoning about going to war and doing what they had to do. This is challenging someone's morality just so you can be curious about what their thinking. This question also screams that you are judging me.

No. 10
Do you feel guilty about what you did during the war?

Would you feel guilty for killing someone who was trying to kill you or threatened your family? Those who serve beside us are our family of choice or circumstance. It might be hard to feel guilty about killing someone trying to kill you or your family. The answer will probably be yes to a point. No one wants to kill anyone or destroy their livelihood. It depends on the circumstance. Combat is chaotic, and why would you even question that? Why would you even bring that up and cause the veteran to go back to that negative emotion?

No. 11
Has any of your friend's committed suicide?

Thank you for reminding me of my losses. Many veterans have lost friends to suicide. I personally have lost 3. When you ask this question, you are making them remember their perceptions of failure. Even though it is not their fault, we all wonder what we could have done differently, and we feel we failed because we could not stop them. People who have loved ones who commit suicide feel the guilt and shame that comes with their perception of failure, so do veterans who have lost friends to suicide. I hear of a veteran suicide at least once a month from a veteran who lost someone from their unit. Please do not ask them to relive their loss.

No. 12
Was the war worth it?

This is asking them if their friends died for nothing. It also asked them if they sacrificed for nothing. These folks left their families to fight for what the government told them was a higher cause. If you had gone to war and sacrificed so much, how you would answer this question.

No. 13
Did you agree with the decision to go to war?

As military members, we have no voice in this decision. Most of us have our opinions, but we often choose not to voice them because it puts us in a precarious position. As a rule, we do not engage in political discussions with strangers. This is a political question.

No. 14
What is it like to be in combat?

It's fun... what the hell do you think. No, really, it is fun to get shot at and bombed. How inappropriate to ask someone to relive some of their fragile moments. Oh! I loved getting shot at. If they answered they liked it, you would think they're crazy because some veterans do like war... and some are crazy. Combat is chaotic, to say the least. Place yourself in a position where you are getting bombed and shot at from all directions. Let us say you are driving down the road and your car is blown up by a bomb. You have family members trapped or dead in the vehicle. When you get out to help your family members, you are shot at by snipers. You are lucky, that probably will never happen to you in the United States, and you have a veteran to thank for that. Please do not ask a veteran to relive some of the worst events of their lives.

No.15
What is it like to be shot at?

Some veterans never see combat, so you are assuming you are talking to someone that has been shot at. I would answer... I do not know why you don't take off, and I will bring out my weapon and shoot at you. Where that might not be said out loud, it might be what their thinking. Asking a person if they have been shot at can bring up a host of negative emotions. It can trigger them if they have been shot at, especially if the shots hurt or killed someone. It can also trigger guilt and shame that comes with being in combat for some. It can also start them questioning their morality, challenging their thoughts on their character.

No. 16
What type of discharge did you get?

Unless you are an employer, a Veteran Service Organization, or the VA, this is none of your damn business. This is a very personal question. The veteran feels less than if he made a mistake and got a dishonorable discharge. I have worked with multiple veterans who were kicked out because they were self-medicating to deal with their PTSD. It is bad enough to send our folks to war; we give them a dishonorable discharge because they tried to survive and made a mistake. It is **not** OK to get mental health help in the military, but it is OK to drink alcohol. I know someone was kicked out after 12 years for a DUI because he self-medicated due to his PTSD from Iraq. Some with PTSD turn to illicit drugs to deal with their pain. I know someone else who received a dishonorable discharge because a recruiter lied to meet his quota for the Marines. The person disclosed his medical issue to the recruiter, who changed it on the official paperwork. The person was kicked out later after serving 3 years because he "lied" on his enlistment medical document. So, you never know why a person might have a dishonorable discharge, and it might not be for misconduct. I am not a big believer in assuming but assume a veteran has an honorable discharge in this instance.

No. 17
Do you have PTSD?

Do you have aids? The same type of question. You are assuming that the veteran you are asking was in combat. On top of that, not all combat veterans get PTSD, and not all veteran's PTSD is caused by war. In a recent study, it was found that only 6% of people with PTSD have it from combat. Most PTSD comes from physical assault and sexual assault. PTSD is so related to the military because the Veterans Administration drives the conversation about PTSD. Also, some people join the military to get out of their situation, which probably involved some type of trauma before they ever entered the military. Also, PTSD has recently been linked to genetics. It can be passed down genetically, just like schizophrenia, bipolar and other ailments. This does not say that folks who get it passed down have PTSD. It just makes them more susceptible to getting it in later life. People are not proud of their PTSD, and asking them if they have it is just not acceptable. Again, it reminds them of the incident that caused their PTSD.

No. 18
Do you get triggered? What are your triggers?

Once someone finds out that a person is a combat veteran, it is possible that they feel safe enough to ask this question. I could see a veteran saying something like, assholes that ask stupid questions are my biggest trigger. You are asking them to tell you their greatest weakness. You are also asking them to open up to how they are internally thinking and their thought process. You are basically asking: What buttons do I push to piss you off. Why would you ask them that? Unless you know them well and want to have a relationship with them, this is not a good question. It could trigger them and turn the situation into a negative experience.

No. 19
Do you have a brain injury? (TBI)

Another stupid question. Because Traumatic Brain injury or (TBI) is the signature injury of the most recent wars, folks think it is OK to ask if someone has TBI. TBI is another one of those hidden injuries like (PTSD). When you ask someone this question, it makes them wonder if they are acting like they are damaged, and if they have a brain injury, it points out to them that it is noticeable. They could feel that you are judging them, causing them to act out. Their injury could cause rage, trigger their anger, or cause them to shut down. It's not good to ask this question. It is like asking you if you are schizophrenic because of the way you are acting. This is a very personal question that should only be asked by a doctor, therapist, or a close family member. By asking them, they can shut down and not want to be a part of society. Often someone with TBI struggles to leave the house because of their injury. When you ask them, it solidifies their thought process and causes them to not want to go out of their home. It could also lead them to thoughts of suicide.

No. 20
Did you get hurt in combat?

Again, you are assuming they were in combat. If you ask this question, it is usually because they are missing a limb or have visible scars. By pointing out their differences, it can remind them of the event. Even if combat was not the cause of their disability, it could remind them that they are different. Asking this question can cause anxiety and the feeling of not being accepted. Most veterans who were injured during combat just want to be treated the same as everyone else. Hell, most folks with disabilities want to be treated equally.

On top of that, most injuries surrounding veterans are not seen. As mentioned above, PTSD and TBI are common unseen injuries. What makes you think that it is OK to ask a question about their disability. If you know someone who is not a veteran but in a wheelchair, do you ask them how they lost their legs? Well, you might if you are that nosey. Unfortunately, people cannot just be quiet and move on.

No. 21
What did your spouse think of you going to war?

This question makes a lot of assumptions. You are assuming they were married, went to war, and are still together. Going to war could have caused the demise of their relationship. My answer would probably be a sarcastic, Oh! They loved me being gone, leaving them alone with two kids. Do not ask them about how their spouses felt. If you are that nosey, ask their spouse so they can tell you their thoughts. Do not be surprised if you get a smart-ass answer from them. What do you think? Do you think they loved their spouse and parent to their children are in a war zone? They were probably scared or worried that they would lose their loved ones and be left alone with children and no one to help them. Most of the time, military spouses are strong. They must be to survive. This can bring up some guilt and shame for the veteran who was deployed. If they were divorced, it reminds them of their perceived failures as a partner and parent.

No. 22
Did your deployment hurt your relationship?

How would you be if you were gone for a year and living in a combat zone? For some families, it secures their relationship and builds a better bond. At times you do not know what it will be like when you get back. Did you trust your spouse while you were gone, or did Jodi visit? Do you trust their spouse now? So, asking a veteran if deployment hurt their relationship can cause a host of negative thoughts. No one goes to war and comes back the same person. With some relationships going to war can help because it causes the veteran to see things differently. When you go to war, your thought process has changed. For some veterans, it causes them to look at what is important differently, helping the relationship. It causes some veterans to change negatively, causing the spouse to not want to be with them. I have also seen veterans leave the relationship because they felt damaged, and their spouses deserved someone better. I have heard spouses say they just want their old spouses back. There are a lot of variables in this question. A lot of it depends if they had a solid relationship before deployment. Please do not ask this question for your curiosity. If they want to talk about it, they will. This question can cover a range of emotions.

No. 23
How did being gone affect your children?

You are assuming again that they had/have children. Well, how do you think it affected them. Being deployed to a war zone just makes their children happy as hell. The truth is it really depends on their age and level of understanding. If the child is young or not born when a veteran deploys, it can interfere with the bonding process. It has been proven that the bonding process starts in the womb. It can negatively affect the relationship for men who were deployed while their child was still in the womb. Once the child is born and an infant being gone still gets in the way of the bonding process.

Toddlers do not understand why their parents left them. They can blame themselves for the absence because they do not understand or know what is going on. Like their younger siblings in their pre-teenaged years, the lack of a parent can cause a lot of anxiety as they start to figure out what is going on. Most of the time, those with teenagers are career military or in the Guard or Reserves. Teenagers have it rough because they do not want anyone to know how they feel, so they do not say anything. A lot of times, they will act out. Teenagers can watch the news and understand what is happening or not watch it because they do not want to deal with the anxiety. In the veteran, this can trigger guilt and shame because they were not there for their children. This is especially true if their child is emotionally struggling or has a history of getting into trouble. It is rude to make them think about their perceived failures.

No. 24
What was it like in X country?

You are assuming they were deployed to a war zone. If in Germany, Japan, or Korea, it might have been fun, and you might get a response. If it was in a war zone, they might have a smart-ass answer like it was a garden party... seriously, do you want them to relive their time in a combat zone? This could be a massive trigger for a combat veteran. You need to earn the right to ask this question. You must give the veteran time to get to know and trust you before they will tell you anything of significance. They might tell you the funny things that happened and deflect the question. This is incredibly inappropriate if they lost someone while deployed, which you will not know unless you know them. Veterans can talk about some of the instances to people they know and other veterans. There is a trust that they will not be judged for what they had to do, but most veterans will not answer this question honestly if they do not know you.

No. 25
Why did you join the military?

This really is not a stupid or inappropriate question, but I think it is essential to understand why people join. There are a lot of reasons that people join the military. Most people think it is due to being patriotic, but that is not necessarily true. Most people who join the military search for a better life or to pull themselves out of poverty. The reason some joined is to get away from the trauma that they had to live with daily. Some join for the college, and some for the insurance. It could cause them to feel some shame and discomfort if they joined to escape their situation. It is possible to not get an accurate answer unless you spend the time to know them.

No. 26
Is it hard to be a civilian again?

We'll let us see... It depends on your definition of hard. Almost all veterans struggle to fit back into society. Most veterans do not feel civilians have the loyalty to their mission veterans do. When I say mission, I mean to the team. Most civilians do not understand the sacrifice it takes to be a team member and do things for the greater good. The military is a collective society where civilian society is one of individualism. One of the most prominent issues veterans deal with is civilians' inability to follow through on what they said they would do and "flaking out" on their responsibility. One of the critical issues is veterans feel civilians usually will not take responsibility for their actions, causing veterans to distrust civilians.

It also depends on what the veteran did in the military. Some veterans had jobs in the military that were quickly transferred into the civilian culture. Those who were infantry have transferable skills that are harder to showcase in a resume. A combat and wartime veteran's experience will be different than that of a peacetime veteran. Were they drafted or volunteered? Some veterans must live with killing someone if they were in combat and live in a society that looks down or praises you for taking a life.

Veterans are reminded of your event every time someone asks a stupid question. So, the answer is YES! It is complicated and different.

No. 27
What was the nastiest or most disgusting thing you saw over there?

Please do not be curious at our expense. If you mean living conditions or societal norms, you might get an answer. But expect a smart-ass answer. It also depends on the person; every person's definition of disgusting is different. For some, it is seeing dead folks. For others, it is picking up body parts or body parts of your friends. For some, it could be mass graves or children being forced to be suicide bombers, or parents being forced to make their children being suicide bombers. For others, it could be the smell of burning flesh, open sewer systems, and dead or rotting livestock and animals. All of this is based on that individual's perception. But at the end of the day, asking this question can remind them of some of the horrors they had to live through, causing them to question themselves and if they do the right thing.

No. 28
What's the worst thing that happened to you over there?

Please don't ask us to relive the worst time in our lives. If you are close enough, you might find out one day... or you might not. There are so many things that can go wrong at war. Part of it is losing a friend and feeling it is your fault, losing a friend to suicide, and feeling like you missed something that could have prevented it. It could be having to shoot a child or a woman to protect yourself and your unit. It could be watching your entire team blown up and knowing you cannot do anything about it. This all depends on your perspective. Why would you ask a veteran to relive something unspeakable just because of your curiosity?

No. 29
Were you happy to come home?

What do you think? But the truth is some are happy to be home, and others are not. There is no correct answer for some combat veterans because it is complicated. If someone had to leave their combat unit because of injury, they might want to be there with their team and buddies to help protect them. Some combat veterans miss the camaraderie and intimacy established in a combat unit. It is even closer when they are in the theatre of operation. That is why many combat veterans like to hang out with their combat buddies and local Veterans Service Organizations (VSO'). Social media has made it a lot easier to stay in touch with their comrades because that can be a double-edged sword. Social media can be a struggle because they can see their brothers and sisters struggling, and they hear about the suicides of their friends. Most are glad to be home, but some miss the combat and the adrenaline rush that goes with it. Of course, they are going to tell you they are happy to be home. If they said they did not want to come home, you might think they are crazy and judge them. They also might want to go back to combat because they feel safer. Many struggles of coming home are the fear of not fitting into society. Veterans can face an uphill battle once they return home. Their community does not understand them, what they had to do, or their mental illness such as PTSD or TBI. If they got a dear John letter or found "Jodi" (a person with whom their spouse or significant other had an affair), they came to visit. At the same time they were deployed, they might want to stay in the combat zone. It might sound like an easy question, but it is complicated.

No. 30
How are you doing since you got out?

This question appears to be harmless, but many veterans struggle when they get out. This question can insinuate there is something wrong with them. If they cannot find a job, it can trigger them, making them feel worse than they do.

A lot of veterans have had trouble fitting into society since they got out. They struggle to find a job because there are so few veterans in a position to hire veterans. After WWII, Korea, and Vietnam, many veterans were hiring veterans to translate their skills. Those prior veterans have retired, leaving few folks in a position to understand them, understand their skills, and give them a chance. Those who have served and, in a position to help veterans know how to handle someone with PTSD or the quirks most veterans have. Interestingly, many non-military folks who hire veterans believe all veterans have PTSD because the VA drives the narrative surrounding PTSD.

Veterans also struggle when reintegrating because most civilians lack integrity and respect and do not follow through on what they say they will do. In the military, veterans know where the line is of acceptable behavior and what is not. It appears that in the civilian sector, the line moves depending on who you are and your position. In the military, everyone follows the same rules and has the same line for the most part. Unless you know the veteran's story, they will probably tell you they are doing OK just to be polite. It is doubtful you will get a straight answer.

No. 31
Did you see the news...?

Often veterans do not watch the news because they get triggered. I have seen it where new veterans were upset because they saw all of what they fought for go away. Especially if they lost someone, they cared about. It has been worsened since the division in our country. So often, they do not want to discuss it. If they're going to discuss it, they will bring it up.

No. 32
Can you believe what the Democrats / Republicans are doing?

It can be dangerous to think all military support one party over the other. Most veterans fly under the radar when it comes to political parties. It is well believed that most military support the Republican party. It's not as many as you would think. As it stands right now at last survey, over 40% of veterans support the Democratic Party. So, if a veteran is a Republican or Democrat is a crapshoot. Especially in today's climate. It appears things are changing. Discussing politics with a veteran you do not know might end up ugly. They have sacrificed for your right to be wrong, and they might let you know it if they disagree with you.

No. 33
Don't Assume Veterans are religious?

Some veterans lose their religious affiliations in combat because of what they must do to survive. Some combat veterans believe they must give up their morality to survive the situation. The enemy knows American's weak points and exploits them to their advantage. That is why some veterans become atheists. They struggle to support a God that will put them in a position of having to kill women, children, and whole families. I can see how a Soldier, Sailor, Airman, or Marine would question their religion and God when they see someone force a child to strap on a suicide vest and run towards them. The enemy does not care if they use Americans' generosity and love of children to blow them up. These soldiers are forced to do something no one should ever have to live with, shoot a child. The enemy also forces women to do the same thing knowing the American mentality about protecting women. Women have also been known to plead for help and draw troops into an ambush. It has been reported that there are about 1/3rd of the active-duty military has no religious affiliation. So yes... there are Atheists in foxholes.

No. 34
What do you think about the U.S. being over there? Do you think we should get out?

This is like asking someone who has sacrificed so much if their losses were worth it. Many veterans have lost loved ones in combat. Asking them if we should be in the war they have been sent to. If you say we should stay, then the veteran opens themselves up for your judgment. If the veteran believes we should get out, it opens the veteran's chance to feel like his losses for nothing. This places the veteran in a precarious position. A military veteran went "over there" on your behalf, and you should appreciate their sacrifice and not ask them to choose a side because of your need to be correct.

No. 35
What do you think about gay/trans folks in the military?

To begin with, the veteran might be gay, lesbian, or transgender. There are over 1 million known LGBT veterans. There are also an estimated 65,000 serving on active duty. Most veterans and active-duty members only care if someone can shoot straight and have their 6. They could care less who they are attracted to. A firearm only knows a good shot from a bad one. The weapon does not care who they are attracted to, and most military members and veterans are the same way. Some veterans are against gay folks in the military, but more do not give a damn than do. This makes you, the person asking, look homophobic. On top of that, why would you care except for being nosey and curious?

No. 36
Can I pet your dog? Or just petting a service dog.

That is like asking a blind man if you can touch his cane. The dog is working when they have their vest on. Please do not ask to pet a service dog. It does not matter if it is a civilian or veteran who has the animal. This is rude and can cause the veteran to be rude to you and tell you no. Then you will huff and be butt hurt! Service dogs are doing a job and keeping their partner safe. By petting the dog, you are distracting the dog. This could cause something to happen to the veteran. It is unlikely but possible. Remember, many folks have vests for their dogs who are not genuinely working dogs. A fully trained working dog will usually be unnoticed and well behaved.

No. 37
Do not say that you had a PTSD moment.

PTSD moments are reserved for those with PTSD, and they're probably not going to say it out loud if they have one. What you are doing is discounting their disability and making fun of people with PTSD. It is bad enough to have the symptoms of PTSD but having to listen to someone flippantly make a comment like that is disrespectful. Folks with PTSD struggle daily in multiple aspects of their life. Why are you going to make fun of them?

No. 38
I know what it is like to go to war

Again, there goes the assumptions, and the truth is. NO, YOU DON'T unless you have been there. End of discussion!

No. 39
Thank you for your service, but I do not think we should have been there.

Well, just shut up then. Saying something like that is like saying thank you for being a scout leader, but I would not let my son join because there are too many sexual predators in the scouts. Save your thoughts for your civilian friends, or better yet, just do not say anything. Do not discount a veteran's service to the country by making a comment like that.

No. 40
My cousin was in in the Army... you might know him

There are over one million people in the Army. That is like saying, oh! You are from Jersey, my cousin lives there, you might know her.

No. 41
I was going to join...but

Our thoughts are usually, well, why didn't you. It does not matter if you were or not. Even if it was a medical issue that kept you out, you did not join at the end of the day. Therefore, your comment is disrespectful. We feel you are trying to take a shortcut to get to know us so you can ask stupid questions.

No. 42
I know how you feel

No, you don't. Unless you have sacrificed relationships, had children while deployed, been through Bootcamp, to war, or have PTSD, you don't. Anxiety, depression, moral injury, are also a hallmark of a combat veteran's struggles. Unless you have been shot at, had to kill someone, or had a fellow military member killed, you don't know how I feel, and I hope you never have to.

No. 43
Do not tell a combat veteran that you understand what they are going through. Then, share a personal/unrelated story.

Please don't go there. Unless you have been in combat, there is no way you can understand. Veterans can talk to each other even if one has not been in battle. A civilian cannot understand what it is like to give away their freedoms to the government, hoping they will do the right thing.

No. 44
DO NOT... even in a joking manner, tell a combat veteran that they should be grateful they made it home alive, did not die, need to get over it, and be happy.

Many veterans lose someone in war if they have seen combat. They might be struggling with the loss of their comrade, they might feel that it is their fault their friend is dead, they might have survivors' guilt. As a civilian, you can't fathom what it feels like unless you have lost a family member in combat. You cannot just get over it!

SEXIST, INAPPROPRIATE QUESTIONS/COMMENTS PEOPLE ASK SPECIFICALLY TO FEMALE VETERANS.

No. 45
Why did you join? the military is a man's job

I will guess one of the answers might be to get away from sexist assholes like you. That is a sexist comment and should not be made to any female who has joined the military. There come back could be, especially if the person answered the question has never served because my balls are bigger than yours. Many female members join to see the world, get away from people like you, get out of a bad situation, go to college, and make a better life for themselves. You know the exact reasons men join.

No. 46
You are a mother/wife. How could you leave your family?

Because it is my job. Why do you travel for your job? Why do you go to work? Why aren't you staying home with your family? Men are not asked this sexist question, so why ask a female veteran.

No. 47
How did your husband/boyfriend feel about you being around all those men?

Men do not get asked this question. My thought is, if my husband/boyfriend does not trust me, then I need a new boyfriend/husband. How would you like it if your significate other told you I do not want you going to your job because there are too many women/men there?

No. 48
Did you join the military to find a husband?

Maybe they did... Perhaps they didn't. What business is it of yours? Contrary to popular belief, women do not go into the military to find a spouse. Do you go to work to find a spouse? Maybe you did... Perhaps you didn't. Why would they be different?

No. 49
I hear all women are sexually assaulted/harassed in the military. Were you?

Where do I start with this? Unless you are their therapist, this is none of your damn business. Men are not asked this inappropriate question, even though men are sexually assaulted in the military too. Why would you choose to bring up a person's trauma if they were? Do you go around and ask civilian women if they have been sexually assaulted? Well, nix that, anyone who would ask this question probably would because all they care about is themselves and their curiosity.

No. 50
I bet you had your pick of men over there.

Yeah, they do, but what makes you think they want a military man. The military is a hyper-masculine environment. Most women do not want the testosterone-driven, macho, sexist mate the military can offer. I am not saying all men in the military is sexist and a testosterone-driven animal. But there is a lot of masculinity and one-ups man ship in the military. Often the truth is revealed in the military. The odds are good, but the goods are odd.

No.51
Women don't serve in combat

Tell that to female combat veterans, and you just might get your ass kicked. Women have been serving in combat since the dawn of time. As a therapist and combat veteran, I have worked with many women who served in the war. Many were in "non-combat roles" but were sent out on convoys in Iraq and Afghanistan, subjected to consistent attacks. The families of the 152 women who were killed in Iraq and Afghanistan would disagree. Of the 152 females who were killed, 84 were slain by hostile fire. On top of that number, over 1,000 women have been injured. Show them the respect they deserve.

Conclusion

Inappropriate questions can cause veterans to be triggered, question themselves, and examine their decisions. A lot of veteran's struggle to assimilate back into society once they become a civilian again. A lot of the struggles veterans face, people do not understand. That is why asking stupid questions can cause an issue for some veterans. Are you going to trigger them by asking stupid questions? It depends. You need to ask yourself why is it OK to take that risk? How veterans react to these questions depends on the situation and where they are in their recovery process, reintegration, or life. Not knowing the veteran, their mental state, or where they are in their psychological state can cause an issue. Remember, they might be in a heightened state when you ask the questions. Flashbacks can be commonplace with some veterans, especially if they do not know or trust you. Just because they are in a location that is in public, such as college, work, or social events, does not make it appropriate to ask questions. Most veterans seem content and docile, but that can change if triggered.

The biggest fear is your questions causing the veteran to think about suicide. When you ask inappropriate questions, it can bring up a host of issues with them. Your questions can cause them to look back and have guilt over multiple issues and decisions they had to make while in combat. Some veterans have guilt over losing someone in their unit. They may feel their decisions caused someone to be killed, even though it was not their fault. The veteran might have guilt over the need to shoot a child to save their own unit. They might have survivors' guilt because someone took an assignment they were supposed to have and were injured or killed because they were sick or injured and could not complete their assigned task. Survivors' guilt is a massive issue for a lot of veterans. I have worked with snipers who had to watch as their whole unit was wiped out, and they could not do anything. When a person feels guilt, they believe that a part of who they are is intrinsically bad. They end up feeling sorry for who they are and who they have become. This can cause them to question their existence, believe they fail, and let everyone down.

Sometimes the questions you ask can bring shame to the veteran. It depends on the veteran and their experiences and the situation. Shame is one of those things a veteran must deal with when you have done something against your morals. Let us say you ask someone who is an Iraqi war veteran if they had ever killed someone. If they killed a child or a woman, they probably wouldn't answer your question and feel shame. Many veterans live with the guilt of what they had to do to make it home alive to their families. They might become triggered by your question, sending them "down the rabbit hole" of despair.

Another thing your questions can cause the veteran to shut down and question everything they have done. When veterans shut down, they keep everything inside, causing undue stress on themselves and possibly their families. This can cause someone to struggle internally with themselves, causing turmoil in all aspects of their lives. Many veterans who have shut down struggle with sleep disturbances. Losing sleep because of nightmares can place them on edge and more likely to do things they usually would not. Rest is one of the most important things we as humans have. The lack of sleep can cause all kinds of problems down the road. Sometimes lack of sleep causes a veteran to lash out and become aggressive.

I have known veterans who thrive on shock value. When asked stupid questions, they will say something like, yep! I loved shooting children; they are smaller and faster targets. It improves my marksmen ship. They might also bring up raping and pillaging to shut you down. You might have no idea what you awoke with your stupid question. So many veterans struggle to reintegrate because of their dark sense of humor. You just provided them an opportunity to whip it out by your ridiculous question. Do not be shocked if a veteran responds with something like this.

Sometimes the inappropriate questions can cause a veteran to feel and think of how stupid and ill-informed you are to even ask that question. It makes you look insensitive and selfish. It makes a veteran feel that your curiosity is more important than their wellbeing. People asking stupid questions are why some veterans do not go out into society, wear military clothing, or show their pride in service. Asking insensitive questions or comments is a part of the there-integration struggle. When you walk up to a veteran you do not know and ask an inappropriate question, you solidify their thoughts that they do not belong in society. They can feel misunderstood. I would suggest that the best thing you could do is spend some time getting to know a veteran, and they might open up to you. You must understand where they are coming from. The best way to think about it is to earn the right to hear their story and ask any questions. Getting to know them is the least you can do for someone who has fought for the rights and freedoms you have today. If they are rude, you might want to look at yourself in the mirror and ask, did I ask a stupid question?

Living the Dream: Nightmares of Military Integration

When military veterans separate from the military, they face struggles that are hard to understand. Finding their place and a purpose is not as easy as it sounds. The military tells us when we separate there will be people waiting in line to hire us because of our dedication, punctuality, loyalty, work ethic, and the desire to get the job done. That is true for some, but others struggle to find a job or friends, and acquaintances, trying to become a civilian again. Living the Dream is intended to let veterans face once they leave Active Duty. It is my hope this book will encourage society to help veterans find their place and a purpose.

Living the Dream II: Nightmares of Navigating the VA System

Veterans struggle with health issues caused by the beatings their bodies and minds take while in the military. Struggling with the VA bureaucracy can be daunting because of the system Congress has set up. Some veterans give up on the VA because it is hard to navigate and frustrating. This book was written to help veterans and their families understand the VA system.

www.ingramcontent.com/pod-product-compliance
Lightning Source LLC
LaVergne TN
LVHW050337160826
845677LV00014B/3652

* 9 7 9 8 4 9 2 1 8 3 7 7 6 *